FREEDOM IN CHRIST

FOR YOUNG PEOPLE AGED 15-18

D1785350

First published in the UK in 2009 by Monarch Books (a publishing imprint of Lion Hudson plc)
Wilkinson House, Jordan Hill Road, Oxford OX2 8DR, England
Tel: +44 (0)1865 302750 Fax: +44 (0)1865 302757
Email: monarch@lionhudson.com
www.lionhudson.com

ISBN 978-1-85424-926-5 (UK) (single copy)

ISBN 978-1-85424-927-2 (UK) (pack of five)

ISBN 978-0-8254-6324-2 (US) (single copy)

ISBN 978-0-8254-6325-9 (US) (pack of five)

Distributed by:
UK: Marston Book Services, PO Box 269, Abingdon, Oxon, OX14 4YN
USA: Christian Market: Kregel Publications, PO Box 2607, Grand Rapids, Michigan 49501

Published jointly with:
Freedom in Christ www.ficm.org.uk and British Youth for Christ www.yfc.co.uk

The text paper used in this book has been made from wood independently certified as having come
from sustainable forests.

British Library Cataloguing Data. A catalogue record for this book is available from the British Library.

Printed and bound in Hong Kong by Printplus Ltd

Contributors: Sara Hargreaves, Bethan Lawler, Phil Knox, Sue Lea
Editors: Steve Goss, Phil Knox, Rich Miller, Simeon Whiting

WELCOME TO FREEDOM IN CHRIST

FOR YOUNG PEOPLE AGED 15-18

INTRODUCTION

TO FREEDOM IN CHRIST FOR YOUNG PEOPLE

HELLO AND WELCOME TO FREEDOM IN CHRIST FOR YOUNG PEOPLE. THIS IS AN AMAZING COURSE THAT WILL CHANGE YOUR LIFE. JESUS CAME TO EARTH AND LIVES TODAY TO SET YOU FREE AND SEE YOU REACH YOUR POTENTIAL TO BE ALL THAT HE HAS MADE YOU TO BE. THIS COURSE IS ABOUT CONNECTING WITH THE AMAZING TRUTH IN THE BIBLE ABOUT WHO YOU ARE AND HOW TO DEAL WITH STUFF THAT CAN HOLD YOU BACK IN YOUR RELATIONSHIP WITH GOD.

This accompaniment is your guide throughout the course. Use it alongside each session to help you get your head around what is being talked about and explored. There are loads of parts to it – important Bible verses, challenges, prayers for you to pray, questions and a journal section each week to write down how the truth is affecting your everyday life and space to write and grapple with questions.

We hope and pray that you get so much out of this course and you get to know God loads better. May you know the truth that will set you free.

✱ NOTE - If you are using this in the USA you will notice that there are a few different spellings!

CONTENTS

LET'S GET STARTED!

KEY TRUTHS

1. WHO WAS I?

WHAT'S THE POINT?

- God designed us to be secure, significant and accepted and we often search for these things in the wrong places.

- When Adam and Eve messed up they lost spiritual life which had given them security, significance and acceptance. Jesus, through his life, death and resurrection, came to restore this to us.

- When we become Christians we automatically become secure, significant and accepted in Jesus even if sometimes it doesn't feel like it.

KEY VERSE

I HAVE COME THAT THEY MAY HAVE LIFE, AND HAVE IT TO THE FULL.

JOHN 10:10

JOURNAL

What the Bible says about who we are in Christ is amazing. What are the truths on the next two pages that particularly stand out to you? Spend this week's journal page writing down the truths that mean the most and how they make you feel.

TRUTHS SECTION

I AM SIGNIFICANT

I am no longer worthless, inadequate, helpless or hopeless. In Christ I am deeply significant and special. God says:

I have been chosen and appointed by God to change the world around me. (John 15:16)

I am a temple of God where God's Holy Spirit lives. (1 Corinthians 3:16)

I am a minister of 'making peace' for God. (2 Corinthians 5:17-21)

I am God's workmanship, created for good works. (Ephesians 2:10)

I may approach God with freedom and confidence. (Ephesians 3:12)

I can do all things through Christ who strengthens me! (Philippians 4:13)

I am part of God's family and I have my role to play. (1 Corinthians 12:27)

I AM SECURE

I am no longer guilty, unprotected, alone or abandoned. In Christ I am totally secure. God says:

I am assured that in every circumstance God works for my good. (Romans 8:28)

I am free from any guilty charges against me from God. (Romans 8:31-34)

I cannot be separated from the love of God. (Romans 8:35-39)

I am sure that the good work God has begun in me will be perfected. (Philippians 1:6)

I am a citizen of heaven. (Philippians 3:20)

I am kept safe with Christ in God. (Colossians 3:3)

I am a child of God and I am safe from any evil. (1 John 5:18)

I AM ACCEPTED

I am no longer rejected, unloved or dirty. In Christ I am completely accepted. God says:

I am God's child. (John 1:12)

I am Jesus' chosen friend. (John 15:15)

I am holy and acceptable to God. (Romans 5:1)

I am a saint, a holy person. (Ephesians 1:1)

I have been forgiven for all the things I've done wrong. (Colossians 1:14)

I am complete in Christ. (Colossians 2:10)

QUESTION FOR NEXT WEEK?

IMAGINE THAT YOU'RE TALKING TO SOMEONE WHO IS NOT A CHRISTIAN. CAN YOU THINK OF A SHORT WAY TO SHARE YOUR FAITH IN A FEW SENTENCES? COME PREPARED TO SHARE YOUR SENTENCES NEXT WEEK.

KEY TRUTHS
2. WHO AM I NOW?

WHAT'S THE POINT?

- We used to be sinners but when we became Christians, Jesus transformed us into saints, children of God.

- Every child of God has a brand new identity and heart but if we believe our old identity of a 'sinner' still exists, that's how we will act.

- We are more than just forgiven by God; we also have his Spirit in us and can live in freedom.

KEY VERSE

IF ANYONE IS IN CHRIST, HE IS A NEW CREATION; THE OLD HAS GONE, THE NEW HAS COME!

2 CORINTHIANS 5:17

JOURNAL

Write down two or three things that have been especially meaningful to you in this session

TRUTHS SECTION

I TURN MY BACK ON THE LIE THAT MY FATHER GOD IS:

- distant and uninterested in me
- stern and demanding
- too busy for me or not there
- impatient, angry or never satisfied with what I do

- mean, cruel or abusive
- trying to take all the fun out of life

- condemning or not forgiving

- looking for faults or expecting me to be perfect

I JOYFULLY ACCEPT THE TRUTH THAT MY FATHER GOD IS:

- close and involved in my life (see Psalm 139:1-18).
- kind and caring (see Psalm 103:8-14).
- accepting of me and is filled with joy and love (see Romans 15:7; Zephaniah 3:17).
- patient and slow to get angry and delights in those who put their hope in his unfailing love (see Exodus 34:6; 2 Peter 3:9, Psalm 147:11).
- loving and gentle and protects me (see Jeremiah 31:3; Isaiah 42:3; Psalm 18:2).
- to be trusted and wants to give me the best possible life! (see Lamentations 3:22, 23; John 10:10; Romans 12:1-2).
- kind and forgiving; His heart and arms are always open to me (see Psalm 130:1-4; Luke 15:17-24).
- wants me to grow and is proud of me (see Romans 8:28; Hebrews 12:5-11; 2 Corinthians 5:17).

QUESTION FOR NEXT WEEK?

DO YOU BELIEVE THAT A PERSON WHO DOESN'T BELIEVE IN GOD HAS MORE OR LESS FAITH THAN A CHRISTIAN? WHAT ABOUT A HINDU OR MUSLIM? OR SOMEONE WHO JUST DOESN'T KNOW?

KEY TRUTHS

3. WHERE DO I PUT MY FAITH?

WHAT'S THE POINT?

- Everyone has faith in something. It's part of everyday life.
- It's not the fact that we have faith. What's important is what or whom we put our faith in.
- We can see from our actions what we really believe. If we trust God, then people will see it in our actions.

KEY VERSE

WITHOUT FAITH IT IS IMPOSSIBLE TO PLEASE GOD, BECAUSE ANYONE WHO COMES TO HIM MUST BELIEVE THAT HE EXISTS AND THAT HE REWARDS THOSE WHO EARNESTLY SEEK HIM

HEBREWS 11:6

JOURNAL

Write down two or three things that have been especially meaningful to you in this session

TRUTHS SECTION

WHAT CAN I DO?

1. Why should I say 'I can't' when the Bible says I can do all things through Christ who gives me strength (Philippians 4:13)?

2. Why should I lack when I know that God will supply all my needs according to his riches in glory in Christ Jesus (Philippians 4:19)?

3. Why should I be afraid when the Bible says God has not given me a spirit of fear, but one of power, love and a sound mind (2 Timothy 1:7)?

4. Why should I be weak when the Bible says that the Lord is the strength of my life and that I will display strength and take action because I know God (Psalm 27:1; Daniel 11:32)?

5. Why should I allow Satan supremacy over my life when he that is in me is greater than he that is in the world (1 John 4:4)?

6. Why should I be depressed when I can recall to mind God's loving kindness, compassion and faithfulness and have hope (Lamentations 3:21-23)?

7. Why should I worry and fret when I can cast all my anxiety on Christ who cares for me (1 Peter 5:7)?

8. Why should I ever not be free from stuff that holds me back knowing that, where the Spirit of the Lord is, there is freedom (2 Corinthians 3:17; Galatians 5:1)?

9. Why should I feel condemned when the Bible says I am not condemned because I am in Christ (Romans 8:1)?

10. Why should I feel alone when Jesus said he is with me always and he will never leave me nor forsake me (Matthew 28:20; Hebrews 13:5)?

11. Why should I be discontented when I, like Paul, can learn to be content in all my circumstances (Philippians 4:11)?

12. Why should I feel worthless when Christ became sin on my behalf that I might become the righteousness of God in him (2 Corinthians 5:21)?

13. Why should I be confused when God is the author of peace and he gives me knowledge through his Spirit who lives in me (1 Corinthians 14:33; 1 Corinthians 2:12)?

14. Why should I feel like a failure when I am a conqueror in all things through Christ (Rom 8:37)?

15. Why should I let the pressures of life bother me when I can take courage knowing that Jesus has overcome the world and its tribulations (John 16:33)?

CHALLENGE

Pick one verse from the 'What Can I Do' list that particularly stands out to you. Write it in the Journal section and say it out loud to yourself every day this week as a reminder of what you can do with God.

THINK

Although we are accepted, secure and significant in Jesus, as Christians we need **faith** to grow. How do we live out our faith? Is it by saying we have faith but behaving exactly the same as always? Or is it by believing and acting on that belief?

PRAY

Father God, you are....

(fill in the space with descriptions of what God is, e.g. 'my Rock')

QUESTION FOR NEXT WEEK

IMAGINE YOU WERE BORN IN ANOTHER COUNTRY; DO YOU THINK THE WAY YOU LOOK AT THE WORLD AND YOUR BELIEFS WOULD BE DIFFERENT?

WHAT ARE WE UP AGAINST?

4. WORLDVIEW

WHAT'S THE POINT?

- We each have a different worldview, or perspective, which can affect the way we see God and ourselves.

- The culture in which we live and our past experiences can affect and distort the way we look at the world.

- We need to choose to look at ourselves and God through a Biblical worldview and not mix and match it with any other perspective that is not as true.

KEY VERSE

I AM THE WAY AND THE TRUTH AND THE LIFE. NO-ONE COMES TO THE FATHER EXCEPT THROUGH ME.

JOHN 14:6

JOURNAL

This week write down all the things that you think influence your worldview. What are you watching/reading/thinking about? As you read the Bible this week how does this affect how you see yourself and God?

TRUTHS SECTION

WHICH WORLDVIEW?

1) How do you make decisions about the future?

a) I read horoscopes.

b) By using logic, common sense and the latest scientific research.

c) By praying and reading the Bible.

d) I don't. Any choice I make is as good as another. I go with the flow.

2) What do you think happens when you die?

a) I will probably be reincarnated.

b) Science tells us that nothing happens, so that's what I believe.

c) I hope I will go to heaven.

d) Who knows, who cares?

3) What do you spend most time reading?

a) Manuals for white magic.

b) My chemistry text book.

c) The Bible.

d) Wikipedia, MySpace and Facebook.

4) Who do you go to for advice?

a) My local witch doctor.

b) My science teacher.

c) God and Christian friends.

d) I don't really need advice.

5) Which of these best describes why you're a Christian?

a) Keeping a cross around my neck scares away the evil spirits.

b) Someone showed me the proof of things like the flood, creation and the existence of Jesus.

c) I believe that Jesus Christ is the only way to God for all people everywhere at all times.

d) What I have experienced leads me to feel that Christianity works for me.'

RESULTS

Mostly a's
You are mostly influenced by an animist worldview.

Mostly b's
You are mostly influenced by a modern worldview

Mostly c's
You are mostly influenced by a Biblical worldview.

Mostly d's
You are mostly influenced by a postmodern worldview.

CHALLENGE

Read the truths from Session 1 again (on pages 8&9).
For every lie you discover the media/your friends/the world is
trying to get you to believe, read one of these and remember
who you are in Christ.

PRAY

Father, thank you that you are the Truth. Help me to look at
life through the truth of your Word and to be wise in what I
look at and read so that so I come to know you as you are.
Amen.

QUESTION FOR NEXT WEEK

IF WE KNOW WE ARE SAINTS, WHY IS IT THAT WE STILL SO OFTEN MESS UP?

WHAT ARE WE UP AGAINST?

5. BIG CHOICES

WHAT'S THE POINT?

- As Christians, our old sinful nature is gone but we still have our old ways of thinking, reacting and coping, characteristics known as 'the flesh', and we have to choose to change.

- We have to unlearn our 'fleshly' way of thinking and learn how to think in line with God's truth – the Bible calls this 'renewing our mind'.

- It's all about choice – we will still be tempted to sin but we can choose to walk by the Spirit and not give in to temptation.

KEY VERSE

YOU, HOWEVER, ARE CONTROLLED NOT BY THE FLESH BUT BY THE SPIRIT, IF THE SPIRIT OF GOD LIVES IN YOU

ROMANS 8:9

Write down two or three things that have been especially meaningful to you in this session

WHAT'S IT TO ME?

What happened to you when you became a Christian?

Using the three characters, Norman, Sam and Fred, describe what your faith looks like at the moment.

NATURAL NORMAN · SPIRITUAL SAM · FLESHLY FRED

What characteristics will you have if your life is full of the Holy Spirit?

Why is walking in the Spirit something you have to choose to do every day?

CHALLENGE

Take five minutes to be quiet with God. Ask him to show you areas of your life where you have not been renewing your mind and are still thinking in ways that are not in line with God's truth. Write these down and make the choice to change.

THINK

As a Christian, does it sometimes seem like you are tempted more than ever to do the stuff you shouldn't? Remember that the Bible tells us the power of sin is broken in our lives (Romans 6:5-18) and we are free now to turn our backs on it and choose freedom.

PRAY

I know that the only way I can do this is by choosing to live by the power of the Holy Spirit in line with your Word. Amen.

QUESTION FOR NEXT WEEK?

ARE THERE SINS THAT **KEEP HAPPENING OVER AND OVER,** THAT YOU KEEP GOING BACK TO, SINS THAT YOU CAN'T SEEM TO STOP COMMITTING? WHY DO YOU THINK THAT IS?

WHAT ARE WE UP AGAINST?

6. STRONGHOLDS

WHAT'S THE POINT?

- Strongholds are deeply ingrained attitudes and actions that do not match the truth of God's Word, the Bible.

- We can renew our minds using the Word of God to get rid of thoughts and attitudes in our heart that aren't true.

- When we choose to believe the truth in God's Word, we will grow and make better choices.

KEY VERSE

WE DEMOLISH ARGUMENTS AND EVERY PRETENSION THAT SETS ITSELF UP AGAINST THE KNOWLEDGE OF GOD, AND WE TAKE CAPTIVE EVERY THOUGHT TO MAKE IT OBEDIENT TO CHRIST

2 CORINTHIANS 10:5

JOURNAL

Write down two or three things that have been especially meaningful to you in this session

....

....

....

....

....

....

....

....

....

....

....

WHAT'S IT TO ME?

Are you aware of any strongholds in your life? If so, list them here.

Why will strongholds stop us growing deeper in our friendship with God?

What has God given us to help us break strongholds down?

Name some choices you can make every day to help you break down strongholds in your life.

CHALLENGE

Sometimes strongholds can be so much a part of us that we are not even aware they exist. Ask God to show you any destructive thoughts and ways of behaving you might have and for the ability to use the truth in the Bible to break them down.

THINK

A stronghold is a thought pattern we have learned, which means it can be unlearned. God wants to get rid of our strongholds so that we can be free to grow with him. Remember that he would never ask us to do anything that is impossible.

PRAY

Lord Jesus, I know that I need to take captive every thought before it takes me captive. Help me to know the truth so well that I can always identify a lie.

QUESTION FOR NEXT WEEK ?

WHAT KIND OF LIES DOES THE DEVIL TELL US?
DO YOU THINK YOU'VE EVER BEEN DECEIVED BY THE DEVIL?

WHAT ARE WE UP AGAINST?

7. SPIRITUAL REALITY

WHAT'S THE POINT?

- Christians are the bull's eye target for the enemy who will try to bring us down by tempting, accusing and deceiving us.

- Comparing Satan's power to God's power is like comparing an ant to an atomic bomb!

- Jesus is far above Satan and demonic powers and because Christians belong to Christ, we have authority over the kingdom of darkness. That is amazing.

KEY VERSE

PUT ON THE FULL ARMOUR OF GOD SO THAT YOU CAN TAKE YOUR STAND AGAINST THE DEVIL'S SCHEMES

EPHESIANS 6:11

JOURNAL

Write down two or three things that have been especially meaningful to you in this session

WHAT'S IT TO ME?

Why are we easier targets for Satan if we ignore the fact that a spiritual battle is going on?

How do we know that Satan is so much less powerful than God?

As Christians, why do we have authority over the devil?

What are the things that we can do to defend ourselves against the devil's temptations, accusations and lies?

CHALLENGE

Can you think of a time when you have felt tempted, accused or deceived? The belt of truth is what we need to expose the lies of the evil one. This week your challenge is to read the book of Ephesians and every day write down one verse that contains a truth that stands out to you.

THINK

Do you know who you are in Jesus? The Bible tells us that God has seated us in the heavenly realms with Jesus and we have his power and authority over the kingdom of darkness. If we stay close to God and don't give in to Satan, he has to get lost when we resist him (James 4:7)!

PRAY

Lord God, sometimes it can be really difficult to be aware of lies but I know that you have given me all that I need to grow as a Christian. Help me to take hold of my freedom by knowing how to resist the devil.

QUESTION FOR NEXT WEEK

IF WE CAN'T ALWAYS TRUST WHAT WE FEEL, THEN WHY HAS GOD GIVEN US FEELINGS AND HOW SHOULD WE REACT TO THEM?

FREEDOM FROM THE PAST

8. HANDLING OUR EMOTIONS

WHAT'S THE POINT?

- Our emotions were created by God and show the deep parts of our character and whether our thoughts line up with the truth in God's Word.

- Be honest with God. He is your closest friend. He can handle any of your emotions and loves you as his child.

- Don't act on how you feel but act on what God says is true.

KEY VERSE

CAST ALL YOUR ANXIETY ON HIM BECAUSE HE CARES FOR YOU. BE SELF-CONTROLLED AND ALERT. YOUR ENEMY THE DEVIL PROWLS AROUND LIKE A ROARING LION LOOKING FOR SOMEONE TO DEVOUR

1 PETER 5:7, 8

JOURNAL

Write down two or three things that have been especially meaningful to you in this session

WHAT'S IT TO ME?

Our emotions are reactions to the way we see the world around us but what if the way we perceive things is wrong?

Sometimes emotions feel like they control us but how can we change our emotions over time?

If we always follow our feelings, will our lives show the freedom Jesus gives us? Why? Why not?

Although useful, we can't trust emotions to be right. What can we trust as truth to base our lives on?

CHALLENGE

How do you handle emotional situations in your life? Next time you are tempted to ignore a problem or emotionally explode, pray and then look at the problem knowing that God will help you deal with it.

THINK

You may have had traumatic experiences in the past that have stuck in your mind and affect your emotions. Your identity is not in the past. It's in Christ and God wants to set you free from everything that holds you back.

PRAY

Lord I know that the only thing I can trust as truth in my life is your Word. Help me not to let my emotions control me but to bring them to you where I can be honest and learn to control them by choosing to believe the truth in the Bible.

QUESTION FOR NEXT WEEK?

THINK OF THE WORST THING ANYONE EVER DID TO YOU. WHY SHOULD YOU FORGIVE THAT PERSON? CAN YOU THINK OF ANY GOOD REASONS WHY YOU SHOULDN'T FORGIVE THEM?

FREEDOM FROM THE PAST

9. FORGIVENESS

WHAT'S THE POINT?

- Forgiveness is about freedom. We forgive so that we can be free from our past.

- When we forgive others we are simply following God's example. He has forgiven us for everything that we have ever done wrong.

- Unforgiveness is one of the biggest ways that the devil has of holding us back in our relationship with God.

KEY VERSE

FOR IF YOU FORGIVE MEN WHEN THEY SIN AGAINST YOU, YOUR HEAVENLY FATHER WILL ALSO FORGIVE YOU. BUT IF YOU DO NOT FORGIVE MEN THEIR SINS, YOUR FATHER WILL NOT FORGIVE YOUR SINS.

MATTHEW 6:14-15

JOURNAL

Write down two or three things that have been especially meaningful to you in this session

WHAT'S IT TO ME?

Does unforgiveness give us freedom or tie us to the person who caused the pain? Why?

Why is forgiveness firstly between you and God?

Is it you or the other person who is damaged more by unforgiveness?

We are forgiven by God. If we don't forgive, what does that say about how much we value God's gift of forgiveness to us?

CHALLENGE

The temptation to hang on to the anger and pain is often so strong but God's love is stronger. As you consider people you have not forgiven, thank God that he gives you strength to do the right thing and then make a choice to forgive them and swap bitterness for God's love.

PRAY

Lord Jesus, I know that I didn't deserve your forgiveness but you gave it to me anyway because of who you are. Help me to be like you and forgive others so I can be free.

When you go through the Steps To Freedom In Christ you will have the opportunity to ask God to show you the people you need to forgive and then to choose to do so by saying:

"**Lord, I choose to forgive** (name of person) _____ **for** (specifically what they did or failed to do)_____ **which made me feel** (verbally tell the Lord every hurt and pain he brings to your mind) _____ ".

There may be people that you want to forgive right now.

QUESTION FOR NEXT WEEK

HAVE YOU GROWN AS A CHRISTIAN AS QUICKLY AS YOU WANTED? IF NOT, WHAT DO YOU THINK IS IN THE WAY?

GROWING AS CHRISTIANS

10. TRUTH = FREEDOM

WHAT'S THE POINT?

- When we first become a Christian, we are a spiritual baby but we need to grow up and become mature.

- We need to take responsibility for what we believe and learn God's truth so that we can uncover any lies we have fallen for.

- Deal with busting strongholds properly and one at a time, not all at once!

KEY VERSE

BUT SOLID FOOD IS FOR THE MATURE, WHO BY CONSTANT USE HAVE TRAINED THEMSELVES TO DISTINGUISH GOOD FROM EVIL

HEBREWS 5:12-14

JOURNAL

Write down two or three things that have been especially meaningful to you in this session

WHAT'S IT TO ME?

How can you take responsibility for growing in your faith so that you become spiritually mature?

What can stop us and what can help us grow as a Christian?

God always wants to help us grow and become more like Jesus. How do we know what he is like? How do we become more like him?

CHALLENGE

Writing and doing a Stronghold-Buster is a great way of getting rid of the lies we believe. Try it out and remember that a stronghold will be stubborn so persevere until it's gone!

The 4 steps are:
1. Uncover a lie you have fallen for 2. Find the truth in the Bible 3. Write the declaration (I turn my back on the lie .../I declare the truth ....) 4. Say it for 40 days

THINK

As Christians we are all part of God's family and we are not alone. Consider asking a mature Christian to help you grow in your faith by challenging and encouraging you.

PRAY

Dear God, I know that my mind is a place that the enemy will try to fill with lies. Help me to learn how to renew my mind, pushing out any lies I believe and replacing them with your truth.

QUESTION FOR NEXT WEEK

WHEN ANOTHER CHRISTIAN DOES SOMETHING WRONG TO YOU, WHAT WOULD BE A GOOD WAY FOR YOU TO RESPOND?

GROWING AS CHRISTIANS

11. LOVING OTHERS

WHAT'S THE POINT?

- Staying close to God and having a good relationship with him should lead to good relationships with others.

- We have two main responsibilities: making sure we do what is right and helping meet others' needs.

- When others are struggling with sin, look to build them up with love and acceptance when helping them walk in truth.

KEY VERSE

JESUS REPLIED: 'LOVE THE LORD YOU GOD WITH ALL YOUR HEART AND WITH ALL YOUR SOUL AND WITH ALL YOUR MIND.' THIS IS THE FIRST AND GREATEST COMMANDMENT. AND THE SECOND IS LIKE IT: 'LOVE YOUR NEIGHBOUR AS YOURSELF.' ALL THE LAW AND THE PROPHETS HANG ON THESE TWO COMMANDMENTS.

MATTHEW 22:37-40

JOURNAL

Write down two or three things that have been especially meaningful to you in this session

WHAT'S IT TO ME?

Does the fact that God loves us no matter what we do make it easier to love other people? Why? Why not?

Why do we naturally focus on our rights in a relationship? How would the relationship change if we focused instead on our responsibilities?

Why does God discipline us and how does it make us better Christians?

What's the difference between judging someone and disciplining them?

CHALLENGE

Encourage at least two people every day this week either by saying something that builds them up or giving them something unconditionally. Take a special interest in those who seem to be on the edge of things.

THINK

Healthy relationships are made up of rights and responsibilities. It can be really easy to focus on our rights. Think about your responsibilities as a Christian to your friends, parents and teachers.

PRAY

I really want to be more like you, Lord Jesus, in the way I treat other people. Help me to put what you want before what I want and always to look to meet other people's needs as you meet mine.

QUESTION FOR NEXT WEEK?

WHAT ARE YOUR GOALS FOR THE REST OF YOUR LIFE? HOW CAN YOU BE SURE THAT YOU WANT THE SAME THING AS GOD FOR YOUR LIFE?

GROWING AS CHRISTIANS

12. WHERE ARE YOU GOING?

WHAT'S THE POINT?

-  God's main goal for you is that you become more and more like Jesus.

- The only person who can stop you achieving this is you!

- God doesn't want us to live in despair but has a plan for our lives that we can fulfil no matter what our circumstances.

KEY VERSE

THE GOAL OF THIS COMMAND IS LOVE, WHICH COMES FROM A PURE HEART AND A GOOD CONSCIENCE AND A SINCERE FAITH

1 TIMOTHY 1:5

JOURNAL

Write down two or three things that have been especially meaningful to you in this session

WHAT'S IT TO ME?

What are your goals for your life?

Why might negative emotions show that we are living with the wrong goals?

What does the world say about what our goals should be and where we put our worth? What does the Bible say?

What's the difference between a Godly goal and a Godly desire?

CHALLENGE

Are there any goals you have that feel really important to achieve in order to feel good about yourself? Are these in line with God's main goal for you of becoming more like Jesus? Write them down and ask God to help you to begin to aim for his goal for your life.

THINK

Do you get angry, anxious or discouraged when you think of what you want to achieve in life and maybe even feel like a failure? God does not want us to feel like this. He has given us a goal that is achievable!

PRAY

Thank you God that your main goal for my life is about my character – what I am like rather than what I do. Please help me focus on simply becoming more like Jesus in everything I think, say and do. Amen.

QUESTION FOR NEXT WEEK

IF YOU FIND OUT THAT YOUR GOALS ARE NOT THE SAME AS GOD'S GOALS FOR YOUR LIFE, HOW EASILY COULD YOU CHANGE WHAT YOU BELIEVE?

GROWING AS CHRISTIANS

13. KEEPING GOING

WHAT'S THE POINT?

- Becoming more like Jesus will involve a choice every day to throw out wrong beliefs and exchange them for the truth.

- God is intimately involved with your life and has plans to give you a hope and a future.

- Don't try to be like someone else! Be the unique person that God has designed you to be.

KEY VERSE

I CAN DO EVERYTHING THROUGH HIM WHO GIVES ME STRENGTH

PHILIPPIANS 4:13

JOURNAL

Write down two or three things that have been especially meaningful to you in this session

WHAT'S IT TO ME?

How do you have fun?

What is the difference between what the world says is significant and what God says is significant?

How do we stay on the right path with God?

Why is Jesus the only person we can put all our trust in?

CHALLENGE

Think about the thing that has most stood out to you during this course, the most important thing you have discovered, and tell someone else this week.

THINK

Where do you look for success, significance, fulfilment, satisfaction, happiness, fun, security and peace? The world directs us in many different and wrong directions. God tells us to look to him and he will supply all our needs.

PRAY

Lord, you have given me all that I need to grow as a Christian and I really want to stay on the right path. Help me always to have your truth as the foundation of who I am and what I do.

FREEDOM IN CHRIST FOR YOUNG PEOPLE **15-18s**

STEPS TO FREEDOM IN CHRIST

THE STEPS TO FREEDOM IN CHRIST

God wants you to be free. The Bible says, **'It was for freedom that Christ has set us free.'** (Galatians 5:1). You may be wondering, "What do I need to be freed from and why?" There is so much stuff that can hold us back in our relationship with God, things that we do wrong (the Bible calls this stuff 'sin'), lies that we listen to about ourselves and about God and attitudes that we hold onto, some from before we were Christians. The reason that God wants you to be free from these things is because he loves you and wants you to know REAL life, not held back by anyone or anything. Jesus said, **'I have come that they may have life and have it to the full.'** (John 10:10).

But sin and the lies that we listen to are serious and can really mess us up and keep us from living this full life that Jesus promises. But Jesus is way more powerful than these lies. And the GOOD NEWS is that when Jesus died on the cross and rose from the dead he broke the power of sin, which means that if we turn to him we don't have to be held back by it any more. And with regard to the lies we may believe, Jesus said, **'You will know the truth and the truth will set you free'**! (John 8:32). God's truth smashes the power of any lies.

We have a choice to make. We need to take time to stop, think, change our minds, turn away from sin and face God once again. This whole process is called repenting, and God alone can give us the strength to do it. Repenting is more than saying sorry. It is actually turning our back on the stuff that we've done wrong. It is like picking up a train from its tracks and putting it back down in the other direction – back to God.

The Steps to Freedom in Christ is a way of doing this. It is not a magical formula, just a simple tool to help you spend time thinking and listening to God about the things in your life you need to rethink and then tell him that you want to live his way. Each step looks at a different area of your life which makes it more manageable, rather than trying to do everything all at once.

It is based on a really powerful verse in the Bible: **'Submit to God, resist the devil and he will flee from you.'** (James 4:7) Give yourself totally to God, stand firm against the devil and his lies and he has to leave your presence. God and the devil are not equal powers. God is so much more powerful and you, as a child of God, have authority, the right and the power, to tell the devil to get lost.

There are a few really important things that will help you get the best out of this time:

- Be honest with God. God knows everything anyway but loves it when his children (you!) come to him and tell it like it is. Don't hold anything back from God – he will not be annoyed with you or reject you because he loves you and accepts you just as you are, no matter what you have been into or what has been done to you.

- Keep asking the Holy Spirit to show you what you need to repent of and sort out. David in the Bible prayed, 'Search me O God and know my heart.' (Psalm 139:23) Trust God to lead you through each step and be open to what he wants to show you.

- You may get nagging thoughts in your mind as you go through this process like, 'this isn't going to work', or 'God doesn't love me'. If you do, choose to believe God's truth, that he DOES love you and wants you to be free.

- Speak the prayers and declarations out loud. God knows what is going on in your mind but the devil doesn't so when you tell him to leave he needs to hear it. It also will help you focus and add conviction to what you are saying. The things you need to say out loud are **in bold print like this.**

Start by praying the following prayer out loud:

Dear Heavenly Father,

Thank you that you love me, that you want me to be free and that you are right here with me. You are the only all-knowing, all-powerful and ever-present God. Please fill me with the Holy Spirit and show me the stuff in my life that I need to look at and get rid of. Please reveal to my mind everything that You want me to deal with today. We ask for and trust in Your wisdom. Help me not to be afraid of what other people may think or anything else. Thank you for the truth in the Bible that sets us free. I choose to believe that truth today. Amen.

Then make this following 'declaration' out loud:

Jesus is the most powerful name in the world and in his name I command Satan and all evil spirits to leave me. You cannot stop me listening to God and getting rid of the stuff that holds me back. In the name of Jesus you have to go.

STEP 1 – Fake v Real

We live in a world that tries to tell us that there is other spiritual stuff that can replace God. This stuff is real and can really mess us up. It can confuse us and make us believe lies about God. Turning to these things instead of God does not please him. So we need to turn our backs on this stuff totally. Every sin that we have not repented of can give the devil a way to hold us back. Sometimes we may have done stuff for a joke or because our friends were doing it, but even then the devil can still use it and we need to tell God we are sorry and turn away from it.

At each step, we will be doing three things:

● Asking God to show us the stuff in our lives that we need to repent of (sin)
● Saying sorry for doing that wrong stuff
● Committing to follow God's truth instead

So let's begin by asking God what he wants to show you in this area of your life:

Dear God, please show me the things I have done that involve spiritual stuff which is dangerous and does not help my relationship with you. I want to be free from the fake stuff and know the real stuff. Amen.

You may already be thinking of things that were weird, confusing or clearly evil that you were involved with. Go ahead and write them down as you think of them. To help you remember, we have a list below of some of the more common bad spiritual stuff that people get involved with. Make a mark in the box next to anything that you have ever experienced and ask God to show you any others that you might have forgotten about as you read them. Take your time. If you have never experienced any of these things, nothing comes to mind or you don't even know what they are, that is great. You can thank God for that! For anything that comes to your mind in this area, pray the prayer at the end of this step to confess and repent of those things.

❏ Anything to do with Satan - including reading books on witchcraft, casting spells, trying to read minds, trying to harm people by using evil power, taking part in any meetings where the devil is important.
❏ Ouija board (pronounced wee-juh or wee-jee)
❏ Anything to do with Satan
❏ Fortune telling
❏ Tarot cards
❏ Séances
❏ Spells and curses
❏ Sexual spirits
❏ Hypnosis
❏ Palm reading
❏ Horoscopes
❏ Superstitions - like good luck charms, amulets, using crystals for protection or energy
❏ New Age teachings, books or practices
❏ Seeking friendship or guidance from angels, spirit guides or imaginary friends
❏ Other similar things:...

People have always been trying to search for God. That is why there are so many different religions. You may even have had family members teach you to follow other religions (such as Islam, Hinduism, Buddhism, etc.) or no religion at all. Jesus, however, said clearly that he is the only way to God. Trying any other way will hold us back. Ask the Holy Spirit to show you if you have been a part of any religion or group that does not believe that Jesus is the only way to God and write it below:

....
....
....
....
....
....
....
....
....
....
....
....

In the media all around us, there is so much stuff that God doesn't like. Not because he wants to stop people having fun but because he loves us and the stuff that we watch and read can really affect us and damage our relationship with him.

If you have watched any films or TV shows, read any books or magazines, played any video or computer games or seen anything on the internet that focused on the devil or were really violent write these below:

....
....
....
....
....
....
....

If you have never been involved in any of the things in this section, thank God for that. But if you have, you now have a list of things that may be holding you back and it's important you turn your back on them and commit to following Jesus and his truth instead. Do that by praying the following prayer for each area of fake or evil spiritual stuff you've been involved in. Say the prayer once for each single one.

Dear God, I am sorry for getting involved in .... and I turn my back on it. Thank you that you have already forgiven me. I choose to follow you instead. Jesus is my Lord. Amen.

The devil is always trying to deceive us and lead us away from God. We don't need to be afraid of him but we do need to be on our guard against him and aware that he wants to get in the way. The next few questions will help us see if there are any other ways we may have given him influence:

Do you have any nightmares that keep repeating?

....

....

Have you ever talked to or listened to a spiritual being apart from God (like an imaginary friend)?

....

....

Have you ever seen aliens or thought aliens were contacting you?

....

....

Have you ever done anything that focused on Satan even if it was just messing around?

....

....

Have you ever felt like there was an evil presence in your room or anywhere else?

....

....

Have you had any other spiritual experiences that have made you uneasy, frightened or disturbed you?

....

....

Again, once you have filled in any answers to the above questions, tell God and turn your back on these experiences by praying the following prayer.

Dear God, I have experienced .... and I turn my back on it. I refuse to let the devil use this to hold me back from my friendship with you. Thank you that I am forgiven and free. Amen.

God says that you are amazing. You are his masterpiece (Ephesians 2:10) and his child (John 1:12). But the devil wants you to believe that you are a loser and that you have to look a certain way or achieve stuff to be loved. Sometimes we can have thoughts like 'I'm stupid' or 'I'm ugly' or 'Nobody loves me', or we can feel dirty inside. We can start to feel worthless or that we can never do anything right or good. All of those thoughts are lies – total rubbish – and the truth is what God says about you.

You may think that those thoughts are just your own thoughts. The devil, however, can mimic your voice as he whispers these thoughts into your mind. Other people can also speak those lies to us and the media around us can tell us that we have to buy certain clothes or do certain things if we want to fit in or be a success. These lies can stick in our minds, and they can really mess up our lives if we believe them. No matter where these lies come from, we need to make a choice not to believe them.

If these or other negative thoughts about you keep coming up, take this opportunity to expose them for the lies that they are. Make a choice to believe what God says, which is, of course, the truth that you are an incredible child of God made in his image and loved just the way you are.

Write down the negative, repeating thoughts you get here:

....

....

....

....

....

....

Now say the following prayer for every single one:

Dear God, I am sorry that I have paid attention to thoughts that are not true, like .... Thank you that you have already forgiven me. I now choose to believe the truth that you love me and that I am an amazing child of God because of what Jesus has done for me! Amen.

Well done. We are nearly through Step One, but there is one final area to look at. Jesus was asked in Matthew 22 what the most important commandment is. He said it is to love God with all of our hearts, souls and minds – everything we have (Matthew 22:37). Next we are going to look at those things in our life that may not be wrong in themselves but that we have made more important than God in our lives. If we've put anything before God in our lives, we need to tell God we were wrong to do this and put him back in first place. First pray that God would show you what you need to sort out and then mark the boxes below for any things that you know have sometimes become more important to you than God.

Dear God, please show me anything in my life that I have made more important than you so that I can put you back in charge. Please guide my thoughts as I think about this. Amen.

The following are some of the more common things that can take God's place in our lives. God may show you others too.

- ❑ Ambition
- ❑ Food
- ❑ Alcohol/drugs
- ❑ Computer games
- ❑ Money
- ❑ Celebrities
- ❑ My youth group or church
- ❑ TV/movies/media
- ❑ Music
- ❑ Any sport (playing or being a fan)
- ❑ Fun
- ❑ My appearance
- ❑ School work and getting good grades
- ❑ Friends
- ❑ Boyfriend/girlfriend
- ❑ My popularity
- ❑ Parents
- ❑ Other similar things:..

Now pray the following prayer for any that you have marked:

Dear God, I am sorry that I have made .... more important than you. Thank you that you are so much better than anything else. Please help me to keep this thing in its proper place in my life. You are number one. Amen.

You have completed Step One – well done!

STEP 2 – Lies v Truth

One of God's qualities is that he is TRUTH. All that he is and all that he says and does is true. Jesus says, 'I am the way the truth and the life' (John 14:6). But we live in a world of lies that trap us and hold us back.

Jesus said 'You will know the truth, and the truth will set you free.' (John 8:32) Believing what God says will change your life and set you free.
We can choose what we believe and where we put our trust. Just because something doesn't feel true doesn't stop it from being true and having the power to change our lives. Sometimes we don't feel something that God says is true but we need to believe it and put our trust in it.

Sometimes we believe lies that other people, the devil or the media tell us. Below is a list of lies we might believe. First ask God to show you the lies that you believe by praying the next prayer and then mark the box next to each lie that comes to mind. Following each lie is the Bible verse that tells you the truth.

Dear God, I know you want me to believe the truth and I believe that this truth can set me free. Please show me the lies that I have believed and help me choose to believe what you say. Amen.

- ❑ Money and owning the newest, coolest stuff will make me happy (1 Timothy 6:10)
- ❑ Lots of food, alcohol and drugs will make me happy (Proverbs 23:19-21)
- ❑ Looking good will make me happy (1 Peter 3:3-4)
- ❑ To be really happy, I need more than what God wants to give me (2 Peter 1:3)
- ❑ I can hang out with people who get involved in bad stuff and it won't affect me (1 Corinthians 15:33-34, Proverbs 4:23-27)
- ❑ Getting involved in sex outside of marriage is ok and will make me happy (Ephesians 4:22; 1 Peter 2:11)
- ❑ It doesn't matter what I do in private; it won't hurt me or anybody else (Hebrews 3:12,13)
- ❑ There are no consequences for the things I do wrong (Galatians 6:7-8)
- ❑ I have to make sure people like me in order to be happy (Galatians 1:10)

It is important that you repent for believing any of these lies, turn your back on them and choose to believe what God says instead. The following prayer will help you to do that. Put any lies you have marked into the blank and pray about them one at a time:

Dear God, I am sorry for the times that I have believed the lie that .... Thank you that you have already forgiven me. I choose to believe the truth you have given us in the Bible. Amen.

Now look up the Bible verse next to each lie you marked and read it out loud to yourself. You may need to keep doing this for a few weeks to replace the lie you have believed with God's truth.

As well as believing lies the world tells us, we can also fool ourselves. Below are some ways in which we can do this. Look at the list and if you think you fool yourself in this way, then mark the box and pray the prayer afterwards, putting the lie in the blank.

- ❑ I can just read the Bible and not do exactly what it says. I can just pick and choose the parts I like (James 1:22)
- ❑ I may make mistakes but I never sin (1 John 1:8)
- ❑ I think I am something/somebody that I am not (Galatians 6:3)
- ❑ I can say whatever I want, even if it hurts somebody else, and still be a strong follower of Jesus (James 1:26)

Dear God, I am sorry for the times when I have misled myself by believing the lie that .... Thank you that you have already forgiven me. I choose to believe the truth you have given us in the Bible. Amen.

When we mess up, sometimes we can act in a wrong way to defend ourselves and to avoid being found out or losing people's respect. When we do these things, we lie to ourselves, or others, and it can end up causing more damage. Below is a list of some of the wrong ways we can use to try and protect ourselves when we mess up. Look at the list and if you think you do any of these things, then mark the boxes and pray the prayer afterwards, putting each thing you marked in the blank.

- ❏ Denying something happened when it did
- ❏ Putting off dealing with it by doing other things first
- ❏ Retreating into a fantasy or virtual world to try and escape what is real and unpleasant
- ❏ Keeping people at a distance so they won't reject you
- ❏ Taking out your anger on other people
- ❏ Making excuses for what you've done
- ❏ Lying to cover it up or shift the blame to someone else

Dear God, I am sorry for the times when I have messed up and then handled it in a wrong way by .... Thank you that you have already forgiven me and that you defend me when I need that. Amen

Great. You are almost through the second step. Truth is amazingly powerful. The Bible says that the Word of God is like a double-edged sword! So we are going to finish this step by unleashing some of that power by saying out loud some amazing truth from God about who he is and who we are in him.

TRUTH DECLARATION:

There is one true God who is alive and who loves me and wants to know me. He is awesome. (Exodus 20:2,3 15:11)

Jesus came to show me the way to live and then died on a cross for me so that my sins could be forgiven and I could have a relationship with God. He rose from the dead and lives in everyone who trusts him to rescue them from sin. (John 3:16; 14:6, 1 Peter 3:18)

I am saved forever by God's grace through faith in Jesus. Through him I am now a child of God and have a place waiting for me in heaven when I die. (1 John 3:1-3, Ephesians 2:8-9, John 1:12; 14:2)

Being saved is a gift from God and not a result of any good things I may do. (Ephesians 2:8, 9)

I choose to be strong in the Lord and in the strength of his might. I have authority to stand against the devil because I am God's child. (Ephesians 6:10)

Knowing God's truth sets me free. The Bible is totally inspired by God and he wants to speak to me and teach me through it, so that I can become everything he wants me to be. (John 8:32, 2 Timothy 3:16)

The greatest thing that God has asked me to do is love him with everything I have and love those people around me. I choose to do that now by God's strength. (Matthew 22:37-39, Ephesians 6:10)

The good news of Jesus is the power of God and will save everyone who believes. It is the only hope the world has. Jesus has told me to take this good news to those around me in what I say and do. I am his representative. (Romans 1:12, Matthew 28:19, 2 Corinthians 5:20)

Jesus has total authority in heaven and on earth and I give myself totally to him. Satan and all other spirits have to do what I say because Jesus lives in me. In the name of Jesus, I tell them right now to get lost and they have to go! (Matthew 28:18, Galatians 2:20, James 4:7)

STEP 3 – Bitterness v Forgiveness

People not forgiving each other is one of the biggest reasons why relationships break down, people leave the church and Christians are held back in their relationship with God. It is so important that we get this forgiveness thing right for the sake of ourselves and everyone around us. The Bible gives three massive reasons why we should forgive:

- God tells us to do it. (Matthew 6:9-15)
- God has totally forgiven us so we need to do the same to others. (Luke 6:36)

- So that we do not give Satan an opportunity to take advantage of us. (2 Corinthians 2:10-11)

Forgiveness is a real challenge, but when it happens it is one of the most powerful things.

Unfortunately, there is a lot of confusion and incorrect teaching about what the Bible says about forgiveness. The following will help you to understand God's definition of forgiveness.

Forgiveness is not forgetting. You won't forget all the hurtful things done to you before you get around to forgiving, so don't wait for that to happen. God tells us to forgive now for our own benefit. The key issue is this: we may not be able to forget our past, but we can be free from it by forgiving others. When we bring up the past and use it against others, we are showing that we have not yet forgiven them (Mark 11:25).

Forgiveness is a choice, a decision that we have to make. Since God requires us to forgive, it is something we can do. Forgiveness seems hard because it pulls against our sense of what is right and fair. We naturally want revenge for the things we have suffered. But we are told by God not to take revenge but leave it to him (Romans 12:19). He can and will deal with them fairly. You might be thinking, "Why should I let them off the hook?" But what most people don't understand is if you don't forgive you are the one who is hooked. Holding resentment and pain over what has been done to you is like having a big hook in your mouth. Forgiving is like letting the person off the hook and then discovering you were the one with the hook in your mouth. Forgiveness is for your own good and you cannot be free without it.

How do you forgive from your heart? You allow God to bring to the surface the pain and hurt towards those who hurt you. Forgiveness needs to be a head and a heart thing, involving our mind and our emotions. Too often we try to bury the pain inside us, making it hard to get in touch with how we really feel. Though we may not know how to, or even want to, bring our feelings to the surface, God does. Let God bring the pain to the surface so that he can deal with it. Be honest with him.

Forgiveness is the decision not to use what they have done against them. When we remember something someone did to us in the past it can be easy to treat them differently. Forgiveness is choosing to let the wrong thing go and not bring it up any more.

> **IMPORTANT: If someone is continually bullying you or abusive in any way, God dosen't want you to keep on suffering. So, as well as forgiving them, you need also to put a stop to what is happening. A good start would be to tell someone you trust , like a parent, teacher or youth group leader.**

Don't wait to forgive until you feel like forgiving. You will never get there. Your emotions will begin to heal once you have obeyed God's command to forgive.

There may be some people in your life that you have not yet forgiven. Spend some time praying, asking God to bring to your mind anyone you need to forgive. Use the prayer below:

Dear God, please bring to my mind right now all of the people who have hurt me, whether they know it or not, so that I can choose to forgive them. Amen.

Once you finish praying, on a separate piece of paper write down the names of people who come to mind and the things that they have done to hurt you. It doesn't matter what they have done – however big or small, however recent or long ago – you need to forgive them to be free. You may need to write your own name down if you have done some things that you regret. If you are angry with God for something, put his name down too. Even though he has never done anything wrong, it is important that you let go of your anger towards him, choosing to trust that he knows what he is doing.

Below is a prayer. Fill in the blanks of who you need to forgive, what they did or how they messed up and how this made you feel. Be honest with God about this. Don't be afraid to use hard words like 'angry', 'furious', 'betrayed', 'alone', 'hateful', 'scared', 'humiliated' and so on, if that's how you feel.

Take your time. Don't rush through this. Pray through this prayer for every person on your list and every memory you have of being hurt by that person.

Dear God, I choose to forgive .... (name the person) for .... (what they said or did that hurt you), which made me feel .... (tell God every hurt and pain he brings to mind).

Well done! You are through the hardest part of the third step. Next, pray this prayer to thank God; ask him for healing where you have been hurt and bless the person you are forgiving.

Dear God, thank you that you forgive me for all the times I mess up. I choose now to forgive other people who have sinned against me and hurt me. I choose not to hold any of these things against these people any more. Please heal me where I have been hurt and bless the people I have forgiven today. Amen.

It is very common, even after taking a lot of time to work through Step Three, that you will find other hurts and other people coming to your mind later. That in no way makes what you did here unimportant. Plus, all through your life you will need to choose to forgive people who hurt you. The difference is that now you know what to do to be free from anger and bitterness. Choose to live a life of forgiveness and you will have made an important choice to live in freedom.

It is also very common to believe lies about God, assuming that he is just like the people in your life that have hurt you. Now that you have made the choice to forgive those people, you may find yourself seeing God in a new light. The following statements will enable you to reject lies and choose truth about God. Read the statements below out loud.

Seeing God the way he really is

I reject the lie that God is far off and not interested in me. I choose to believe the truth that God is right here with me and he cares about every part of my life. (Psalm 139:1-18)

I reject the lie that God is mean, cold or uncaring. I choose to believe the truth that God is warm and kind-hearted (Psalm 103:8-14; Isaiah 40:11)

I reject the lie that God is stern, demanding and unforgiving. I choose to believe the truth that God accepts me as I am, forgives me when I sin and is filled with joy and love toward me. (Romans 15:7; Zephaniah 3:17; Luke 15:17-24)

I reject the lie that God cannot be trusted to take care of me or protect me. I choose to believe the truth that God cares deeply about me and will be my provider and defender (Psalm 18:2,3; 1 Peter 5:7; Philippians 4:19)

I reject the lie that God is impossible to please and that he is critical and disapproving of everything I do. I choose to believe the truth that God is committed to my growth and proud of me as his growing child. (Romans 8:28,29; 2 Corinthians 7:4; Hebrews 12:5-11)

I reject the lie that God is trying to take all the fun out of life. I choose to believe the truth that God wants to give me a full life and that his will is just right for me. (John 10:10; Romans 12:2)

STEP 4 – Rebellion v Obedience

It may seem cool to be a rebel and refuse to listen to or obey the authorities over us. We have lots of people who are in charge of us in different ways, from parents to teachers to the government who make the laws we have to obey (even youth leaders!). The Bible says that we should respect our parents (Exodus 20:12) and others in authority over us (Romans 13:1-7). Those verses from Romans even say that God has put those authorities in place over us. We may not always agree with the way that they exercise their authority, thinking that they are denying us freedom and making bad decisions, but showing them love and respect is what Jesus asks us to do. If we don't we can allow another way for the devil to hold us back.

Three notes on authority:

● You don't have to keep being obedient if the person in authority is abusing that authority or acting beyond their authority. If someone in authority is abusing you, physically, verbally or sexually, get help!

● If someone in authority is forcing you to disobey God's laws, then don't listen! God's authority is more important than anyone else's, so obey him.

● Don't think, however, that you have God's permission to disobey authority just because they are telling you to do something you don't like! At times like that obedience can be hard, but God will give you the strength to obey if you ask him.

Begin this step by praying the following prayer and asking God to show you any ways that you have rebelled against parents, teachers or other authorities over you.

Dear God, I have sometimes not been obedient to parents, teachers or other people in authority. Please show me when I have rebelled against them and against you. Amen.

Look at the list below and mark the box next to anyone you know that you have been rebellious towards:

❏   The Government – breaking the law in any way, stealing (including illegal downloading), littering, damaging property, breaking driving laws, etc.

❏   Parents or step-parents – including staying out too late, not doing chores, ignoring them, saying bad things about them behind their backs

❏   Teachers or other staff at school

❏   Youth leader or church leader

❏   God

Pray the prayer below for each box you have marked and each authority that God showed you you've disrespected or rebelled against.

Dear God, I am sorry for the times when I have rebelled against any authorities and not respected my parents, teachers, youth leaders or you. I'm sorry for .... (say what you've done that was disrespectful or rebellious). Thank you that you totally forgive me. I choose to be obedient to anyone in authority over me. Amen.

STEP 5 – Pride v Humility

Pride is a killer. Pride says, "I can do it. I don't actually need God, I am independent enough to do it on my own". The truth is that we absolutely need God and we desperately need each other. Proverbs 3:5 says, 'Trust in the Lord with all your heart and lean not on your own understanding.'

Humility is confidence properly placed in God. We are to be "strong in the Lord and in the strength of his might" (Eph. 6:10). God loves humility and hates pride. The Bible even says that God opposes the proud, but gives grace to the humble (James 4:6). Don't be opposed by God but receive his grace.

There are lots of ways that we can be proud. Pray the prayer below to ask God to show you these areas in your life:

Dear God, I know that I cannot live without you but sometimes I think I am more important than you and other people. Please show me the ways in which I do this. Please open my eyes to all the ways pride controls me. I want to be like Jesus, full of God's strength but deeply humble and caring. Amen.

Look at the list below and mark any ways in which you are proud:

- ❏ Wanting to do what I want more than what God wants me to do
- ❏ Not listening to what God wants me to do but deciding things for myself
- ❏ Relying on my own abilities instead of asking God to help me
- ❏ Always doing what I want to do rather than helping others
- ❏ Thinking that I don't need anyone else's help, including God's
- ❏ Not admitting when I am wrong
- ❏ Bragging about things I have done to make sure people know how great I am
- ❏ Being more concerned with pleasing other people than with pleasing God
- ❏ Getting angry when I don't get the credit I think I deserve
- ❏ Thinking I am a better Christian than other people
- ❏ Thinking that I am more important than other people
- ❏ Thinking that I am better than other people because of what I can do or how smart I am
- ❏ Other similar things:..

It is important to say sorry for these things and choose to be humble. Pray the prayer below for each of these things you have marked.

Dear God, I am sorry for the ways that I have been proud, especially .... Thank you for forgiving my pride. I put all my trust in you and choose to put you and other people before myself. Please give me the strength to do that. Amen.

We live in a world full of lots of different types of people. Some who act or dress differently, some from different races or ethnic groups than us, some who listen to different music or who speak differently. God's love breaks down barriers that divide people. Read carefully the following verses:

For Christ himself has brought peace to us. He united Jews and Gentiles into one people when, in his own body on the cross, he broke down the wall of hostility that separated us. He did this by ending the system of law with its commandments and regulations. He made peace between Jews and Gentiles by creating in himself one new people from the two groups. Together as one body, Christ reconciled both groups to God by means of his death on the cross, and our hostility toward each other was put to death (Ephesians 2:14-16).

Prejudice and hatred have destroyed relationships in the human race. It is still a massive problem in the world today. We might have some attitudes that mean that we treat certain groups of people differently.

Pray the following prayer and ask God to search your heart to see if you have any of these attitudes:

Dear God, please show me if there are any wrong ways in which I look at people who are different from me. Is there anyone I mistrust, fear or think isn't as good as me, just because they are different? I want to treat them the way you would. Amen.

Now write down any particular people that came to mind and then pray the prayer below, putting what you wrote down in the blank.

....
....
....

Dear God, I am sorry when I have thought about or treated .... badly just because they are different from me. That is wrong and I turn my back on it. Please forgive me and help me to treat people as Jesus would. Amen.

Well done. You are through Step 5 – just Steps 6 and 7 to go. Keep going!

STEP 6 – Imprisonment v Freedom

The next step to freedom deals with the sins that have become habits in your life. Many Christians get caught in a cycle like, 'mess up – confess it – mess up again – confess it again – mess up again etc.' Whatever the sin is it can really hold us back from God and he wants to break that cycle. There are three very important things we need to do if we are to break free:

- Repent fully. It can be really easy to just say sorry without actually turning our back on the sin. Repentance leads us to say a definite and determined, 'That stuff is wrong and I am NOT going to be held back by it any more.' Then turn to follow God wholeheartedly and give every area of your life to him.
- Resist the devil. Know that the devil will try and tell you lies about yourself and the sin to encourage you to give in. Know God's truth and choose to believe it and use it as the powerful weapon that it is against him.
- Get a friend to help you out. James 5:16 says, "Confess your sins to one another and pray for each other, so that you may be healed. The effective prayer of a righteous man can accomplish much." Find someone you trust and be honest with them and ask them to challenge you and keep you accountable. Don't feel like you have to deal with everything alone.

Are there any sins that you just can't seem to get away from? Pray the prayer below and ask God to show you these things in your life.

Dear God, I know that I mess up and am not perfect in the things I do and say and think. Please show me the things I need to get rid of so I can be free from sin's hold over me. Amen.

Below is a list of some of the stuff that we do that can imprison us, but that God wants us to be free from. Read the list and ask God to show you what you need to say sorry for, turn your back on and follow God's way instead. If God brings anything to mind that isn't on the list, write it down at the bottom:

- ❏ Stealing (including illegal downloading)
- ❏ Fighting/Arguing
- ❏ Being jealous or envious
- ❏ Complaining
- ❏ Gossip
- ❏ Swearing
- ❏ Being too lazy
- ❏ Lying
- ❏ Hatred
- ❏ Anger
- ❏ Drinking alcohol illegally/taking illegal drugs
- ❏ Other addictions

- ❏ Being greedy
- ❏ Cheating
- ❏ Hurting yourself in any way (like cutting yourself)
- ❏ Trying to take your own life
- ❏ Letting fears control you (eg fear of certain people, fear of death, fear of failing)
- ❏ Other similar things:..

Now for each box that you marked, pray the following prayer, filling in the blank:

Dear God, I am sorry for the times I have sinned by .... Thank you that you forgive me. Please set me free from being imprisoned by sin. I reject the devil's lies and I choose to live your way. Please help me to keep going. Amen.

God has created sex as a great thing to be enjoyed in the safe boundaries of a married relationship. When we are involved sexually with another person outside marriage or view or listen to sexually graphic material, it harms us and is not pleasing to God. Pray the prayer below and ask God to show you any way(s) in which you have used your body sexually outside of God's best for you.

Dear God, I know that you see everything I do and you know what is right and wrong. Please show me now all the wrong ways I have used my body sexually. I want to be clean and free. Amen.

For each thing that God brings to your mind, pray the following prayer:

Dear God, I am so sorry that I was involved with .... (name the activity). That was wrong and I turn my back on doing it any more. Thank you for forgiving me and making me clean through Jesus. I ask you to break off any harmful connection with .... (name the person if someone else was involved). Amen.

In addition to sexual things that we actively choose to be involved in, sometimes people can do things to us sexually against our will (like sexual abuse or rape). These things can bring a huge amount of shame and we can even feel very dirty because of them even though Jesus has made us clean. When someone uses you sexually against your will, you are not guilty of sin, but what they did can still have a lasting effect that hurts you. Pray the prayer below to ask God to show you if there is anything in this area.

Dear God, has anyone ever done anything to me sexually against my will? Please bring to my mind anything that I need to be free from today. Amen.

For each thing that God brings to your mind in this area, pray the following prayer:

Dear God, I want to be clean and free from any harmful effects of sexual sin done against me. I say that the devil cannot torment me any more because of ....(name what was done to you) and I ask you, God, to break any sinful connection with .... (name the person). I make the choice to forgive him/her for doing that to me and I say that I am now free in Christ from their sin. Amen.

The following prayer is a great way to commit to following God totally with our whole body. Pray it after you cannot think of anything else that you have done wrong (or anyone has done wrong to you) sexually:

Dear God, thank you for cleaning me up and cleaning me out through and through. I am not dirty but clean in your eyes. I choose to accept myself as clean as well. And I choose by your strength from this day forward to wait until marriage to be involved sexually. I give myself totally to you. Amen.

IMPORTANT: You may have other issues that trouble you. Maybe you have had an abortion or struggle with drug or alcohol abuse. We have prepared some specific prayers you can pray that your youth leader can download from our website. Please ask for these if you need them.

Once you've prayed about every sin you can think of that was holding you back, finish this step by praying the following prayer to give over this whole area of your life to God.

Dear God, thank you that your commandments are not there to stop me having fun but to protect me from the sin that messes me up and holds me back from you. Please give me a hunger for your Word, the Bible. And as I read it, I pray that you will help me love you more and love sin less. Amen.

You are nearly there. Just Step Seven to go.

STEP 7 – Curses v Blessings

Over the last six steps we have dealt with all sorts of sinful stuff you have done that holds you back from God. But did you know that some of your problems with sin were inherited? Many times we are greatly affected by the sinful actions and attitudes of parents, grandparents, and even older generations. You are not guilty for their sins, but some of their sinful tendencies have been passed down to you. Exodus 20:4-6 talks about sin and curses lasting through generations of families, and it is possible that something like that may be affecting you.

As you look at your family tree, certain patterns may show up. Divorce may be a big problem. Or alcohol or drug abuse. Or anger. Or fear. Or too much focus on money. Maybe it is even occult or satanic practices. But we do not need to be scared. If anything like this is affecting us, God can deal with it.

In this step you are going to ask God to show you if there is any sin in your family's history that is affecting you. Then you are going to spend some time with God, breaking the power any of this stuff has over you. So pray the prayer below and ask God to bring to your mind anything that might hold you back.

Dear God, please show me anything that my family before me might have messed up with or struggled with that affects me now. I want to be free from those things and live in freedom as you want me to. Amen.

Now write down anything that God brought to your mind. It's worth writing down everything that comes to mind even if you're not sure whether it happened or not.

....

....

If there were any attitudes or actions that came to mind, you can turn your back on them and resist the devil so that these things cannot hold you back, because you are a child of God. The prayer below declares that if anything your family has done had a hold over you, that hold is now broken. Pray the prayer for each of the things you wrote down:

Dear God, because I am now in your family and you have thrown out the old stuff in my life and made everything new, I turn my back on the wrong things in my family's past that may affect me. I specifically turn my back on .... I am God's child and in the name of Jesus, I tell the devil to leave me and my family alone. These things can no longer affect me or hold me back in my friendship with God. Amen.

Fantastic! You are almost there! We are so proud of you for your courage in going through these steps. We can imagine that some parts were pretty tough for you. We hope you are already experiencing a new freshness in your walk with God, though you are very likely feeling quite tired!

It's really important now that you continue to stay free of all the stuff you have turned your back on today. Here are a few ways you can do this which are really important in your relationship with God:

- Keep hanging out with other Christians, whether at your youth group or church or at home, and encourage each other.
- Keep being honest with God and pray to him regularly. Relationship is about communication. Tell him how you are feeling and how great you think he is. He loves it when his children want to talk to him. And when you sin, come to God quickly to say you are sorry and turn away from that sin.
- Relationship is also about listening. We can listen to God in two main ways. 1) Read the Bible regularly. It is God's truth and it will feed your heart and mind and set you free. You will also be able to spot the devil's lies a lot easier if you know the truth better. 2) Spend time in silence focusing on God and listening to him.
- Think about good stuff. Philippians 4:8 says to think about things that are true, pure, noble, right, lovely, admirable, excellent and praiseworthy. Let this 'filter' guide you in the music you listen to, the books and magazines you read, the websites you visit, the video games you play, and the TV shows and movies you watch. If any negative thoughts come along, ask God to help you defeat them and think about good stuff (like truth from God's Word) instead.

As we prepare to finish, thank God for what he's done for you today;

Dear God, thank you that you love me enough to die for me and set me free from the stuff that holds me back from you. Thank you for helping me face my sin today. Help me to live for you and give all that I have to you. You are amazing. Amen.

A fitting conclusion to these steps is to speak out the truths about who you are in Christ. Turn to pages 8 and 9 and do that now!

IT IS FOR FREEDOM THAT CHRIST HAS SET US FREE

GALATIANS 5:1